Wings
and Tails

Written by Catherine Baker

Collins

a long, thick tail
• .:: ▬ ▬.▬ .:.▬

a rock high up

a long, thick tail

a rock high up

feet on a long rail

a big wing

feet on a long rail

a big wing

a bee with light wings

a pink bud

a bee with light wings

a pink bud

✿ Review: After reading ✿

Use your assessment from hearing the children read to choose any GPCs, words or tricky words that need additional practice.

Read 1: Decoding

- On page 3, point to the word **high**. Ask: Can you point to the trigraph that makes the /igh/ sound? (*igh*). Turn to page 10 and ask the children to find and read the word with the same sound. (**light**)

- Ask the children to read these words. Can they find the digraphs in the words?

  bee (*ee*)   **wing** (*ng*)   **feet** (*ee*)   **long** (*ng*)   **rail** (*ai*)

Read 2: Prosody

- Go back over the book and discuss the pictures. Encourage the children to talk about details that stand out for them. Use a dialogic talk model to expand on their ideas and recast them in full sentences as naturally as possible.

- Work together to expand vocabulary by naming objects in the pictures that children do not know.

- Ask the children to describe the fox, gull and bee using their own words. Prompt with questions such as: What colour is it? Can you name the other parts of the body? Are they long or short?

Read 3: Comprehension

- Ask the children to point to and describe the objects in the picture on pages 14 and 15. Use words from the text to ask questions: Can you find a **wing/tail/bud/bee**? What is **long/thick/high up/big/light/pink**? Extend by using opposites, such as What is **short/thin/low/down/small/heavy**?

- Can you think of other animals that have wings and tails? Can you think of some things that are NOT animals that have wings or tails? (e.g. *aeroplanes*)